Maria Luisa Londoño Arrubla
Breach of Trust in Comparative Law

Studies on Comparative Law

Volume 2

Breach of Trust in Comparative Law

by

Maria Luisa Londoño Arrubla

SOCIETAS 2013

Bibliographic information published by the Deutsche Nationalbibliothek

The Deutsche Nationalbibliothek lists this publication in the Deutsche Nationalbibliografie; detailed bibliographic data are available in the Internet at http://dnb.dnb.de.

Bibliographische Information der Deutschen Nationalbibliothek

Die Deutsche Nationalbibliothek verzeichnet diese Publikation in der deutschen Nationalbibliographie; detaillierte bibliographische Daten sind im Internet über <http://dnb.ddb.de> abrufbar.

Societas Verlagsgesellschaft KG, Bad Frankenhausen, 2013
Alle Rechte vorbehalten / All rights reserved

ISBN 978-3-944420-04-2

www.societas-verlag.de
www.societas-publishers.com

I would like to express my gratitude to my family for their unconditional support.

Abstract

With the purpose of understanding the strong influence that English trust law has had in Latin America's legislation, this text will develop around the breach of trust in comparative law, contrasting the fiduciary figures in the Common Law and the Civil Law systems, from the study of one of the leading cases in English law that would represent a reference point for the particular analysis of English law and Colombian law, and which study will examine their key similarities and differences.

The role of the history is essential to understand the way both fiduciary figures developed in the Common and Civil law, hence it is integrated with the comparison in this study. Issues such as transplanting law or rules from one system to another are mentioned, since the institution of English trust has been developed in many Hispanic-American countries – including Colombia – despite of coming from a Roman legal tradition.

An important part of this study, will be the differences of the fiduciary figures as a result of the significance of equity in the English law and its strong influence in trust law, which explains the distinct elements with the Colombian equivalent. For this reason, the latin *'fiducia'* is not exactly as the English trust, it has been adopted clinging on the legal traditions country-specific. However, understanding the way they have developed is fundamental, with the globalisation it has become a need to find the unification of business instruments in the Commercial Law that has become increasingly towards the unification.

Maria Luisa Londoño Arrubla

Table of Contents

Abstract 7
A. Introduction 11
B. The Breach of Trust: A reference point for
   English and Colombian law 15
C. The origin of Trust in Common Law and Civil Law 19
   I.   Antecedents of the Roman 'fiducia' 19
   II. Antecedents of the English Trust 23
D. General Differences about the trust in English law
   and Colombian law in relation to the trust business 27
   I.   The simultaneous existence in the English law 27
   II.   The existence of a contract of trust in Colombian law 31
   III. Delegation of Trustee's powers 33
   IV.   Duty to avoid conflicts of interests and not to earn
         unauthorised profits 35
   V.   The Principle of Good Faith 37
   VI.   The Trustee's liability 39
   VII. The validity of exclusion of liability clauses in
         English law 43
   VIII. Remuneration for the performance of the trustee . . 45
   IX.   Duty of the trustee with the trust property 47
E. Comparisons 51
F. Conclusions 53
G. Reference List 57

A. Introduction

The English trust as *'the legal relationship created – inter vivos or on death – by a person, the settlor, when assets have been placed under the control of a trustee for the benefit of a beneficiary or for a specified purpose'*[1] draws nowadays major attention even in civil law countries[2], where a certain number of laws have found inspiration on it. This study will be developed within the framework of commercial law, with particular emphasis on the analysis of the breach of trust in comparative law. A comparison will be made between English law and Colombian law, as the later regardless of being a code based system whose legal tradition has been influenced essentially by the Roman law, has adopted the trust law from English law.

To begin, we will have a practical scenario, taken from one of the leading cases of 'breach of trust' in English law *Foskett v McKeown (2001)*, which will be explained in the first section of the text, and later developed through all its content, so it will provide a key reference point for the explanations of the existence of trusts and trusts law in English and Colombian law, and for exploring their similarities and differences with one another. The purpose of this, is to study the different approaches of English and Colombian law in this specific area of trusts – when the trustee commits breach of trust or there is some kind of wrongdoing by a fiduciary that equity will regard as being equivalent with a breach of trust – and starting from a factual perspective, the former case will be useful to illustrate some of the situations that make trust law different in the English and Colombian legal systems.

---

[1] J Mowbray, L Tucker, N Le Poidevin, E Simpson and J Brightwell, *Lewin on Trusts* (18th edn, Sweet & Maxwell 2011) 1-01.
[2] P Lepaulle, *Tratado Teórico y Práctico de los Trust* (Editorial Porrúa SA 1975) 1.

The rationale of studying not only the current law, but also the way that history of trust developed in both systems, and the way they differ from each other; is that it is not possible to transplant the law of trust from the English Law by identifying it immediately with the Colombian legal equivalent *'fiducia'*. For better understanding, it is necessary to analyse them both in their own context and purpose. As in some way the English trust has been adapted to the Colombian legal system. This is why in various points of the text I will be talking about identifying transplanting considerations, that is, the transplanting of rules between legal systems[3], and the development of the fiduciary figures in both systems from the history to these days, will be conducted in one of the chapters of this study.

In terms of undertaking this project of analysis of English law and Colombian law and examining their key similarities and differences in so far as the concept of the trust is concerned, in English law, when studying the law of trust, it is vital to bear in mind the role of law and equity since *'there is still a body of rules of equity which is distinct from common law rules, and acts as an addition to it'*[4]. This is a big difference between the two legal systems, since Colombia has a civil law tradition that does not make that distinction. As a consequence of this, one of the main points that make trust law different in the two countries, is that in Colombia or any other country with a Civil Law legal tradition is not possible to think of the division of ownership[5] that can occur in the Common Law due to the existence of equity. This will be later outlined in the study along with the main differences of both fiduciary figures.

At this point, it is important to set out and explain the distinct elements in both legal systems that will become central to this work as its analysis progresses. Some of them are: the contract of trust existent in Colombia, the duties of the trustee that refer to the principle of good faith and avoiding conflicts of interest, the trustee's liability and exception of liability clauses contained in the case law, among others. This segment of the text is the one that explains all the legal differences in the fiduciary figures. as the text so far is suggesting, the question that interests us here is whether the trust and its parallel

---

[3] J Ellis, 'General principles and comparative law' [2011] EJIL 22(4), 949.
[4] C Elliot and F Quinn, *English legal system*, (11th edn, Pearsons 2010) 123.
[5] RM Goode and E McKendrick (eds) *Commercial law* (4th edn, Penguin 2010) 42.

figure in the Colombian legal system '*fiducia*' can be understood within the theory of fiduciary business. This is because, as suggested above, the institution of the trust, stripped of the characteristics of English law has been developed in many Hispanic-American countries where it has been regulated in all their relations by special laws, usually with the name of '*fideicomiso*'[6].

In this sense, the English trust, has had a strong influence on Latin America's legislation and has been adopted by the majority of countries[7]. Even when it is not possible to entirely align together the fiduciary figures in Anglo-Saxon and Latin law, since each of them have their very own idiosyncrasies, characteristics and culture of the social groups where they were developed[8].

This text argue that when there is a breach of trust, both systems present certain advantages to protect the beneficiaries; although the English system protects them in a special way since the beneficiaries and the trustee are simultaneously owners on the trust property[9]. The equitable ownership, which is the one the beneficiaries have in the English law confers them the actual enjoyment of the rights in the trust property[10], and I believe that this proprietary status gives them a higher degree of protection than in Colombia where they do not have it.

---

[6] JB Jordano Barea, *El Negocio Fiduciario* (JM Bosch Editor Barcelona, 1959) 32.

[7] MA Carregal, *El fideicomiso: Regulación jurídica y posibilidades prácticas* (Editorial Universidad de Buenos Aires 1982) 36.

[8] JA Arrubla Paucar, *Contratos Mercantiles Tomo IV* (Biblioteca Jurídica Diké 2009) 140.

[9] J Mowbray, L Tucker, N Le Poidevin, E Simpson and J Brightwell, *Lewin on Trusts* (18th edn, Sweet & Maxwell 2011) 1-06.

[10] NP Gravells, *Land law: text and materials* (Sweet & Maxwell 2010) 253.

B. The Breach of Trust: A reference point for English and Colombian law

The analysis will now commence with an examination of one key case relating to breach of trust in English law. This will be used to develop a practical case scenario, which will provide the basis for exploring the differences of trust law in the Common Law and the Civil Law, more specifically in the English and Colombian law. The case will be mentioned through the content of the text. The other sections, regarding the history of trust and the distinct elements of the trust in the English and Colombian law, are the explanation for whether a case like this one given certain circumstances shall have a different treatment in both legal systems or not.

If there is a breach of trust in English law, the beneficiaries are entitled to take action against the trustee[11]. At this point it is essential to bear in mind that the trust in English law is not a contract and when the trustee commits breach of trust this has a different treatment than when there is breach of contract. In Colombian law, we will be talking about breach of contract, as a trust is a contract. This is a major difference between both systems that will be explored comprehensively in Chapter C.

The leading case on the subject of breach of trust in the English law that will be further analysed in this study as mentioned afore, is the case of *Foskett v McKeown*. What follows now is a brief overview of the factual context of this case, and thereafter its legal significance. In this case, the trustee Timothy Murphy, controlled a company that

---

[11] J Mowbray, L Tucker, N Le Poidevin, E Simpson and J Brightwell, *Lewin on Trusts* (18th edn, Sweet & Maxwell 2011) 39-67.

was acquiring land in Algarve Portugal, to develop it and sell it to purchasers. The breach of trust took place when Murphy who held the money on trust, paid the two last instalments of his life insurance policy with trust money that he wrongly stole from the purchasers' trust money, subsequently he committed suicide after paying the fifth premium, and the insurance company paid his family £ 1 million under the policy[12]. This lead to a confrontation between Murphy's children and the purchasers who claimed to be entitled to participate in the same fund.

The idea was to carry out the development of the land with villas and a golf country club. 220 prospective purchasers entered into transactions, however the land was never developed, and when it was time to refund the money to the purchasers they noticed that the money was dissipated. Murphy had taken £ 20,440 for paying his insurance; as a result of this, all of the investors, claimed from Murphy's children the 40% of the insurance policy as a proportionate share. In their defense Murphy's children, alleged that they would have received the entire sum of the policy as a consequence of the payment of the first installments that came from Murphy's own resources, and the payment of the last installments that was made with the trust money did not improve the entitlement of them, therefore, the purchasers were not entitled to any interest or if so, only to the return of the sum misappropriated with interests[13].

The Court of Appeal by a majority decided that the purchasers were entitled only to recover the money that was stolen from them to pay the last premiums with interest, but they were not entitled to a share on the policy, for the impossibility of tracing into the policy moneys[14]. The purchasers appealed, claiming minimum a 40% of the policy moneys pro rata, and the children cross-appealed to uphold the decision of the Court of Appeal reaffirming that the purchasers had no right on the policy moneys. The purchasers noted that it was possible to trace the stolen money through the bank accounts.[15]

By a majority of the House of the Lords it was held that the purchasers had a right over the insurance policy in proportion to the value which they contributed to it allowing the appeal, – Lord Steyn and Lord

---

[12] Foskett v McKeown [2001] 1 AC 102 (HL).
[13] Ibid.
[14] Foskett v McKeown [1998] Ch 265; [1998] 2 WLR 298 [1997]; 3 All E.R. 392 (CA).
[15] Ibid.

Hope dissenting, limiting the trust beneficiaries to a lien for £ 20,440 – and dismissing the cross-appeal. This decision represented that financial recovery by way of tracing, which the process of identifying the trust money that the trustee wrongfully mixed with his own, was to be pursued on principles of proprietary entitlement. As the purchasers found a way of tracing those sums, the court decided that the policy moneys were held in trust for the children and purchasers in proportion of their contributions.

Lord Millet held that *'where a trustee wrongfully uses trust money to provide part of the cost of acquiring an asset, the beneficiary is entitled at his option either to claim a proportionate share of the asset or to enforce a lien upon it to secure his personal claim against the trustee for the amount of the misapplied money'*[16]. The beneficiary according to this has two options and can decide the cause of action that finds most beneficial for him. This case is a triumph of proprietary interests of a beneficiary claimant over those of other claimants.

If this case was to be decided according to Colombian law, the decision will be that the purchasers have no rights to the moneys of the policy, they will have the right to recover their money the one that the trustee deliberate stole from them and the interests, although that will not entitle them to have a share in the policy. The decision in a Colombian court would be similar to the Court of Appeal decision in *Foskett v McKeown*, albeit by a different mechanism. According to the Colombian legislation, in this case the trustee acted fraudulently we will be in front of a case of fiduciary liability for intentional mishandling[17]. An action for damages would focus to argue that there was a wrongful act attributable to the trustee which caused harm and there is a causal link between the wrongful act and the damage[18].

In Colombia, the trustee will be responsible for any loss of the trust property only if the liability necessarily result from a breach of contract[19]. According to the Colombian Commercial Code the trust assets must be kept separate from the rest of the assets of the trustee and from those corresponding to other trust business, and form a separate estate subject to the objectives specified in the constitutive act[20]

---

[16] Ibid. by Millet LJ.
[17] Article 63 Civil Code of Colombia.
[18] Article 1613 Civil Code of Colombia.
[19] JA Arrubla Paucar, *Contratos Mercantiles Tomo IV* (Biblioteca Jurídica Diké 2009) 163.
[20] Article 1233 Commercial Code of Colombia 1971.

whose sole purpose is the fulfillment of the trust management. To this point the trustee incurred in breach of contract, as in the English law in breach of trust at the moment of taking the trust money for his personal expenses.

An important difference is that the decision in English law is recognising the property interests of the beneficiaries, which they could enforce by following the asset or by tracing the value of the property[21]. This is an advantage from the perspective of the beneficiaries in comparison with the Colombian solution, as they will have the security that if the trustee stole the trust money it is possible to recover it although he no longer has it. This does not mean that in Colombia the beneficiaries would not have this possibility; it is possible to pursue the assets until certain point especially if the trustee has acted illegally but this would be through different means since they do not have property interest on the trust property, they have a mere expectation.

Before directing this introductory overview to the project more extensively to the comparative approach there is more preparatory work to be undertaken. It is now important to integrate the history of trust to the study in order to understand the way that the law developed in both legal systems and have a clearer view of the significance that English trust has had in Civil law legislations, this will be introduced in the following chapter.

---

[21] Foskett v McKeown [2001] 1 AC 102 (HL).

C. The origin of Trust in Common Law and Civil Law

To achieve an understanding of the trust concept and how it works, it is necessary to understand how it developed. Therefore, the idea of this section is to give a brief tenure in the history of trust in the Common Law and the Civil Law. This will clarify what the trust is today, and the reason for it being adopted and introduced in Latin American countries, despite their Roman legal tradition.

From exploring this history we will be able to understand, how the Roman system developed a trust in testamentary terms; while the English system developed the trust '*inter-vivos*' this is, when the settlor – the one that creates the trust – is still alive. This justifies the strong influence that English trust has had in countries ruled by the Civil Law, that has lead them to incorporate it in their regulations and codes. This requires us firstly to consider the origins of the Roman '*Fiducia*' on account of its significance for contemporary Colombian law.

I. Antecedents of the Roman 'fiducia'

To achieve correct interpretation criteria and better understanding of the history and development of the Latin '*fiducia*' in Roman law, it is necessary to stress that in the Roman law there were two major fiduciary business: (i) '*Fiducia*' which is an act inter-vivos[22], and (ii) '*Fideicomiso*' which corresponds to the law of succession[23]. With this first clarification we start the historical analysis of the Roman fiduciary figure, where both will be explained in more detail.

---

[22] MA Carregal, *El fideicomiso: Regulación jurídica y posibilidades prácticas* (Editorial Universidad de Buenos Aires 1982) 21.
[23] Ibid., 19.

C. The origin of Trust in Common Law and Civil Law

Originally, the classic roman '*fiducia*' did not imply a transfer of property in the sense that it has today, depending on the purpose of the contract, this could be given to ensure a payment or to acquire a greater degree of protection of the assets. It was based in the good faith 'bona fides'[24]. In fact the word '*fiducia*' in Latin means faith. The owner trusted to the transferee the 'use' of the thing, for the purpose of guarantee or for the purpose of safeguarding it, but with the intention of getting it returned once met these objectives[25]. On account of these different purposes two modalities were presented: (i) *Fiducia cum amico*, and (ii) *Fiducia cum creditore*.

The *fiducia cum amico* is the trust business of custody or administration[26]. It is in the interest of the settlor or a third party beneficiary[27]. The person who was in the need to transfer to another administration of property itself, preferred to transfer the domain to allow a greater capacity to act against the assets. Against third parties, the trustee was the owner of the thing and as such he used to act[28]. The *Fiducia cum creditore* occurred when the obligor was required by the creditor to ensure the debt with a thing – as a guarantee – with the possibility of getting it returned with the payment[29]. This was a sophisticated figure that was intended to provide a guarantee to the creditor[30] and was given in the interest of the trustee who is the creditor whose credit is to ensure[31].

The legal figure of the Roman law, known as '*fideicomiso*' was another form of trust business known in the Roman system, this institution corresponded to the inheritance law, where a person entrusts another the transmission of his estate or part of it to a third person[32];

---

[24] J de Arespacochaga, *El trust, la fiducia y figuras afines* (Marcial Pons Ediciones Jurídicas y Sociales SA Madrid, 2000) 17.

[25] Idid.

[26] JA Arrubla Paucar, *Contratos Mercantiles Tomo IV* (Biblioteca Jurídica Diké 2009) 134.

[27] JB Jordano Barea, *El Negocio Fiduciario* (JM Bosch Editor Barcelona 1959) 21.

[28] JA Arrubla Paucar, *Contratos Mercantiles Tomo IV* (Biblioteca Jurídica Diké 2009) 134.

[29] Ibid., 133.

[30] J de Arespacochaga, *El trust, la fiducia y figuras afines* (Marcial Pons Ediciones Jurídicas y Sociales SA Madrid 2000) 17.

[31] JB Jordano Barea, *El Negocio Fiduciario* (JM Bosch Editor Barcelona 1959) 21.

[32] MA Carregal, *El fideicomiso: Regulación jurídica y posibilidades prácticas* (Editorial Universidad de Buenos Aires 1982) 21.

this figure evolved in the medieval times. The feudal organisation in medieval Europe was characterised by the primogeniture, an institution of Civil law which sought to perpetuate the family and the ownership of certain goods through the line of succession of the eldest son[33]. With the end of the Feudal system and the crisis of the primogeniture, inheritance trusts became important as a way of avoiding inheritance dispositions that contained many disabilities to inherit, ensuring that the goods of the deceased had the destination he desired[34].

Therefore, the fiduciary substitutions as we know it nowadays in the Civil Law countries have their roots in Roman Law, in this subject, the English law had great Roman influence as well[35]. In Roman succession law, there was a requirement to give part of the heritage to certain heirs – the offspring – so use of '*fideicomiso*' to get around that and give property to the person that the settlor wanted to give it to, above the legal dispositions that were setting different disabilities or other means for the cause of heredity. With the same purpose will be used in feudal times.

According to this, historically speaking, the law of trust in Roman law had a special development in inheritance law with the aim of being able to avoid compulsory legal dispositions in favour of certain inheritors, like in the primogeniture system[36]. These trusts were forbidden in the French revolution influencing the Spanish law[37], where its legal and doctrinal growth was affected for said reason, but in the English system they did not have this sort of prohibition. Therefore, in modern law, the law of trust in Common Law systems have many years more of development than in the Roman system[38].

Unfortunately the economic role played by the '*fideicomiso*' in its early stages, to serve as a tool to avoid probate legal provisions, was followed by generalisations that disqualified the trust as a licit business and prevented the development of their potential in countries with laws

---

[33] Ibid., 35.

[34] JA Arrubla Paucar, *Contratos Mercantiles Tomo IV* (Biblioteca Jurídica Diké 2009) 142.

[35] C Sherman, 'The Romanization of English Law' [1913-1914] 23 Yale LJ 318.

[36] MA Carregal, *El fideicomiso: Regulación jurídica y posibilidades prácticas* (Editorial Universidad de Buenos Aires 1982) 21.

[37] JA Arrubla Paucar, *Contratos Mercantiles Tomo IV* (Biblioteca Jurídica Diké 2009) 142.

[38] MA Carregal, *El fideicomiso: Regulación jurídica y posibilidades prácticas* (Editorial Universidad de Buenos Aires 1982) 36.

of Roman roots[39]. I hold that in the English law Henry VIII banned trusts to prevent people from avoiding taxes[40] and they found a creative way to create new types of trusts instead to get around with the legal ban[41], in the Roman law the prohibition of trusts had different reasons as preventing the causative from circumventing the laws that were in favour of the heirs that were not the firstborn, protecting their probate rights. This could be explained because one of the reasons why the testamentary trust was created, was the diversity of disabilities that embodied the Roman law to inherit, so when the settlor wanted to benefit someone that lack of capacity to inherit could use this discretion to impose his will[42].

One important difference between the systems is that at the beginning in the Roman law, the trust was basically based in the good faith of the trustee, and there was no action to enforce it, until people started to abuse and a legal instrument was created to prevent them from this[43]. That lack of proportion between means and end does not happen in the English trust, where the trustee cannot abuse the property that receives, for the reason that he shall share its rights with the beneficiary[44]. Before the regulation of the '*fiducia*' in the Colombian Commercial Code that took place in 1971, the application of the figure was made with reference to the doctrine of comparative law, including, obviously Anglo-Saxon practices on trust[45].

Colombia has a legislative origin, grounded on the 'code based law'. Being a civil law jurisdiction, it was strongly influenced by the French Civil system (Napoleonic Code) and the Italian and Spanish legal traditions[46]. The most important codes for the study of trust are the Civil Code and the Commercial Code, as for all the matters that are

---

[39] JA Arrubla Paucar, *Contratos Mercantiles Tomo IV* (Biblioteca Jurídica Diké 2009) 142.

[40] The Statute of Uses (27 Hen 8 c 10).

[41] G Moffat, *Trusts law: text and materials* (Cambridge University Press 2009) 41.

[42] MA Carregal, *El fideicomiso: Regulación jurídica y posibilidades prácticas* (Editorial Universidad de Buenos Aires 1982) 20.

[43] Ibid.

[44] Ibid., 30.

[45] JA Arrubla Paucar, *Contratos Mercantiles Tomo IV* (Biblioteca Jurídica Diké 2009) 143.

[46] A Ramirez and H Otero 'An Introduction to Colombian Governmental Institutions and Primary Legal Sources' [2011] Globalex (New York University School of Law).

not resolved by the Commercial Code, the provisions of the Civil Code shall be applied[47].

The '*fiducia*' as we know it today in the Colombian law is a triangular process, in within this we find the person of the settlor, who is the one interested in further operation of many that are possible with the support of the commercial trust and therefore will transfer the relevant assets to the trustee, a legal entity authorised by the State[48] to act as such and is subject to monitoring by the State and a third party who is the beneficiary of the management with the mechanism of trust, whom may be even the same settlor or another person or persons[49]. The creation of an autonomous estate is one of the attractions of the trust business, with this; the trust assets form an autonomous patrimony, whose sole purpose is the fulfilment of trusteeship[50]; this legal concept was established under certain limitations, and conditions thus the settlor could recover his ownership[51].

II. Antecedents of the English Trust

For a better understanding of the origins of English Trust, it would be essential to study as well the foundations and nature of equity as well. As this is the main difference between the fiduciary figures in the Civil and the Anglo-Saxon systems that are being object of study.

The case law brings a definition of Equity, in *Lord Dudley v Lady Dudley*, Cowper LC held '*equity is no part of the law, but a moral virtue, which qualifies, moderates, and reforms the rigour, hardness, and edge of the law, and is an universal truth; it does also assist the law where it is defective and weak in the constitution*'[52]. It is not only a set of rules that are different from the Common Law; it acts with it, shaping it.

For Alastair Hudson; Equity is a part of English Civil law that can be understood in three different ways: (i) as a means to ensure that the common law and statutory rules are not manipulated resulting in

---

[47] Article 822 Commercial Code of Colombia 1971.
[48] Article 1226 Commercial Code of Colombia 1971.
[49] JA Arrubla Paucar, *Contratos Mercantiles Tomo IV* (Biblioteca Jurídica Diké 2009) 144.
[50] Article 1233 Commercial Code of Colombia 1971.
[51] Judgement of the Supreme Court of Colombia, 15 of July 2008. Referencia: C-1100131030061998-00579-01
[52] Lord Dudley v Lady Dudley [1705] Prec Ch 241, by Cowper LJ.

an unfairness when being applied to a particular case[53], (ii) as a compilation of substantive principles developed in the Courts of Equity[54], (ii) the procedural rules and forms of action developed by the Courts of Chancery under the authority of Lord Chancellor[55].

In English law, Equity plays an important role in property and the creation of trust. The trust enables more than one person to have rights in the same property simultaneously[56]; this has been considered the most important part of equity and greatest achievement performed in the field of jurisprudence[57]. At this point we can emphasise this as a significant difference with Colombian legislation, where only the trustee is recognised as an owner[58].

From the roots of equity, the trust evolved in the English law in relation to property[59]. The birth of the trust occurred in the 12th century at the time of the early religious wars fought called 'crusades' when christian noblemen from Europe travelled to the Middle East[60]. Many of those men would not return to England in many years, or maybe ever, and a title by conveyance would help them to protect the position of their families[61], and equity would enforce this arrangement[62].

The crusaders wanted to ensure that they would be able to recover all the rights on the property when returning from the war, and as a consequence of this, the idea of the division of property appeared[63]. The crusader was treated as the owner of the land by the Courts of Equity, and the other person that was in charge was treated as the owner of the land by the Common Law Courts[64]. This is how two different owners have property rights on the same thing at the same time[65].

---

[53] A Hudson, *Equity and trusts*, (6th edn, Routledge-Cavendish 2010) 4.
[54] Ibid.
[55] Ibid., 5.
[56] R Pierce, J Stevens and W Barr, *The law of trusts and equitable obligations* (Oxford University Press 2010) 11.
[57] A Hudson, *Equity and trusts*, (6th edn, Routledge-Cavendish 2010) 41.
[58] Article 1226 Commercial Code of Colombia. 1971.
[59] S Wilson, *Todd & Wilson's textbook on trusts* (10th edn, Oxford University Press 2011) 16.
[60] A Hudson, *Equity and trusts*, (6th edn, Routledge-Cavendish 2010) 41.
[61] S Wilson, *Todd & Wilson's textbook on trusts* (10th edn, Oxford University Press 2011) 17.
[62] Ibid.
[63] A Hudson, *Equity and trusts*, (6th edn, Routledge-Cavendish 2010) 42.
[64] Ibid.
[65] A Hudson, *Equity and trusts*, (6th edn, Routledge-Cavendish 2010) 42.

A judicial definition of trust is introduced in *Wilson v Lord Bury* when the distinction between trust and contract is made, Lord Brett held '*A trust, in the most enlarged sense in which that term is used in English jurisprudence, may be defined to be an equitable right, title, or interest in property, real or personal, distinct from the legal ownership thereof*'[66]. English trust can be defined as the act where one person called settlor, gives the control and administration of certain assets to another person called trustee, with the final purpose to benefit a beneficiary[67]. In the English law, a trustee must be a person capable of taking or holding the legal estate, and it is desirable that he should possess natural capacity and legal ability to execute the trust and be resident within the jurisdiction of a court of equity[68].

The English trust has the following characteristics: '*(a) the assets constitute a separate fund and are not a part of the trustee's own estate; (b) title to the trust assets stands in the name of the trustee or in the name of another person on behalf of the trustee; (c) the trustee has the power and the duty, in respect of which he is accountable, to manage, employ or dispose of the assets in accordance with the terms of the trust and the special duties imposed upon him by law*'[69].

It has become apparent that the history plays an important role in what we can understand for trust law in both legal systems today, with its differences and similarities, analysing them bearing in mind the context where they developed. This facilitates the understanding of the reasons whereby it becomes difficult to adopt a legal figure from the English law to bring it to Latin American countries like Colombia that have a different legal system and tradition. This leaves us facing the topic of transplanting law which consists in using and adopting rules between legal systems, from one system to the other.

There are some issues that arise from this transplanting process, like the relation between the law and the culture that has been mentioned through this study. A legal figure like trust, could be adopted from the English law in Colombia, but in practice, its application will be given according to the Colombian legal traditions. There is a bond between law and society that plays a key role in the way that people accepts

---

[66] Wilson v Lord Bury and Others [1879-80] LR 5 QBD 518 by Brett LJ.

[67] J Mowbray, L Tucker, N Le Poidevin, E Simpson and J Brightwell, *Lewin on Trusts* (18th edn, Sweet & Maxwell 2011) 1-01.

[68] Ibid., 2-13.

[69] Ibid., 1-01.

C. The origin of Trust in Common Law and Civil Law

and comply with the law, when a law is transplanted from a different legal system, the relationship with the law is not the same.

The effects of transplanting rules from one system to another cannot be controlled or prevented, this is a controversial subject. For Jaye Ellis '*The embeddedn,ess of legal rules in a culture dooms to failure any attempt to boil a rule down to its essence: when legal cultures learn from one another, they do not take up essences but living cultural artefacts*'[70]. In the article the author stress the difficulties of transplanting a rule from a different system that has been developed in a different culture, which in the new culture is never going to be something familiar, it will be something unknown and alien that they would need to get adapted to.

---

[70] J Ellis, 'General principles and comparative law' [2011] EJIL 22(4), 949.

D. General Differences about the trust in English law and Colombian law in relation to the trust business

Conceptually there is a common root of the Latin *'fiducia'* and the English trust as both can be subsumed under a common rubric of fiduciary business based on loyalty. However, there are certain characteristics of each figure that confers them separate apparent peculiarity from that generic set.

The case *Foskett v McKeown*[71] mentioned in chapter A, will be brought to all the aspects where is pertinent in this section, and if there are other important differences beyond this, will be as well illustrated with cases of English or Colombian law. The purpose of this, will be to exemplify the majority of the theoretical components; hence, if there are situations that may occur, and are not especially covered by this case but are considered important as distinctive elements in both legal systems, these will also be developed in this section of the text. The differences will be studied below:

I. The simultaneous existence in the English law

One important characteristic that differs from the English trust to other similar legal forms, and for this particular study to the Latin *'fiducia'*; is the recognition of the existence of two different categories of the right of property, that falls simultaneously on the same thing, where the trustee is considered the owner in law, and the beneficiary the owner in

---

[71] Foskett v McKeown [2001] 1 AC 102 (HL).

equity[72]. This compels the trustee to act entirely on the best interest of the beneficiary[73]. That separation of ownership confers the trustee legal title and the beneficiary equitable title on the property settled on trust[74], and from this moment it is possible to talk about equitable interest[75].

In *Westdeutsche Landesbank Girozentrale v Islington BC* Lord Browne-Wilkinson held that '*A person solely entitled to the full beneficial ownership of money or property, both at law and in equity, does not enjoy an equitable interest in that property. The legal title carries with it all rights. Unless and until there is a separation of the legal and equitable estates, there is no separate equitable title*'[76].

It is necessary to distinguish the equitable interest and the equitable title. The interest is denoting the quantum of the right to the asset, and the title refers to the strength of that right against others[77]. In the English law many interests can only subsist in equity, as the range of interests that exist in equity is greater than the range of legal interests[78].

When the settlor in a trust arrangement makes a declaration to create a trust in favour of the beneficiary, there is a transfer of title from the owner to the trustee, if the latter has the conscience of hold property as owner at law on behalf of the owner in equity that would be the beneficiary[79], or self-declaration to transfer but the settlor becomes the trustee. There is a conscientious obligation that allows equitable rights to be embodied in existent legal titles[80]. The trust may confer on a beneficiary the equitable ownership of a trust asset, or a partial equitable interest in the asset[81].

The way of transferring and acquiring property in equity, may be by creation of a trust, either (i) by the transferor declaring himself to

---

[72] J Mowbray, L Tucker, N Le Poidevin, E Simpson and J Brightwell, *Lewin on Trusts* (18th edn, Sweet & Maxwell 2011) 1-06.

[73] A Hudson, *Equity and trusts*, (6th edn, Routledge-Cavendish 2010) 41.

[74] Westdeutsche Landesbank Girozentrale v Islington BC [1996] AC 669.

[75] Ibid.

[76] Ibid. by Browne-Wilkinson LJ.

[77] C Elliot and F Quinn, *English legal system*, (11th edn, Pearsons 2010) 44.

[78] Ibid.

[79] A Hudson, *Equity and trusts*, (6th edn, Routledge-Cavendish 2010) 8.

[80] KJ Gray and SF Gray, *Elements of land law* (Oxford University Press 2009) 822.

[81] J Mowbray, L Tucker, N Le Poidevin, E Simpson and J Brightwell, *Lewin on Trusts* (18th edn, Sweet & Maxwell 2011) 1-06.

be a trustee for the intended transferee, or (ii) by transfer of the assets to a third party to hold as a trustee for the intended transferee[82]. Equitable title to property involves divided ownership[83]. These two titles to property, at law and in equity existing simultaneously in the same property, are called simultaneous existence[84].

In the Colombian law, this operates in a different way. It is not possible to assure that the English trust is the same that the Latin '*fiducia*', since expressing its equivalence would provide as a result the inconvenience of combining the solutions contained in two legal systems of hard harmonisation. According to the Colombian law, the transfer of the assets from the settlor to the trustee does not cover the fullness of the domain, only the necessary for the trustee to fulfil the purpose of the trust[85]. The legal nature of the property that the trust confers to the trustee is merely a complete and absolute ownership in order to fulfil the request contained in the agreement.

For that reason, the settlor can retain some rights. In Civil Law countries, there is a role for the settlor in the life of trust. According to the Italian academic Maurizio Lupoi in his comparative study of trust, the law in the majority of civil law systems does not '*imposes limits at the powers which a settlor may wish to reserve to himself in the trust instrument: most describe their reservations of rights on various occasions as a limit to the otherwise free exercise of the fiduciary powers*'[86], considering this in a context which sees the fiduciary as full owner that shall not have any sort of interference of the settlor but to the fiduciary purpose of the relationship[87]. This is also mentioned in the Colombian Commercial Code, that in one of its provisions states that the settlor is entitled to all the rights that he has retained directly to exercise them on the trust assets[88].

In the Civil Law systems, the trustee appears as the sole owner of the asset transferred, and the settlor reserves his mere rights '*in per-*

---

[82] RM Goode and E McKendrick (eds) *Commercial law* (4th edn, Penguin 2010) 43.

[83] Idid., 42.

[84] S Wilson, *Todd & Wilson's textbook on trusts* (10th edn, Oxford University Press 2011) 1.

[85] JA Arrubla Paucar, *Contratos Mercantiles Tomo IV* (Biblioteca Jurídica Diké 2009) 150.

[86] M Lupoi, *Trusts: A Comparative Study* (Cambridge University Press 2001) 312.

[87] Ibid.

[88] Article 1236 n1 Commercial Code of Colombia 1971.

sonam' against the trustee being in obvious lack of protection against the trustee[89]. This imbalance does not occur in the trust due to cleavage of the property mentioned afore.

Applying this first difference to the case that has been our basis, *Foskett v McKeown*[90] it stands out that equity plays a vital role, it is for this division of property that the beneficiaries of the trust who are the purchasers, feel entitled to equitable proprietary rights to 40% of the insurance policy, the English law on equitable principles enables them to claim a proportionate part that was paid with the stolen money and they indicate that they could trace the money[91], ergo they can identify it.

In the Colombian law, the approach will be different, as mentioned in chapter A, the trustee clearly breached the contract of trust according to the Colombian Code of Commerce. Even though, the beneficiaries in Colombia are not owners of the trust property, they have rights provided by law according to which they shall require from the trustee the faithful performance of their duties and to establish the liability for breach of these[92]. Concluding, in Colombia they are entitled to recover the money and interests but not to a pro rata share on the policy.

I hold that the English approach has better protection for the beneficiary, since due to the simultaneous existence he is an owner of the property. The Colombian law does not leave completely unprotected the beneficiary, he has the right to demand from the trustee the compliance with its obligations,[93] although, he does not have a title on the property, the only one that appears as an owner is the trustee. In England and Wales the beneficiary has the option of choosing to follow the assets and this is a great advantage well recognized in the case law in *Foskett v McKeown* where Lord Millet held '*where one asset is exchanged for another, a claimant can elect whether to follow the original asset into the hands of the new owner or to trace its value into the new asset in the hands of the same owner*'[94].

---

[89] J de Arespacochaga, *El trust, la fiducia y figuras afines* (Marcial Pons Ediciones Jurídicas y Sociales SA Madrid 2000) 22.
[90] Foskett v McKeown [2001] 1 AC 102 (HL).
[91] Ibid.
[92] Article 1235 n1 Commercial Code of Colombia 1971.
[93] Ibid.
[94] Foskett v McKeown [2001] 1 AC 102 (HL), followed by Sinclair Investments (UK) Ltd v Versailles Trade Finance Ltd [2011] 3 WLR 1153.

II. The existence of a contract of trust in Colombian law

In the differences between the Roman *'fiducia'* and the English trust, we can point out the fact that the former required a bilateral pact, while the latter was generally constituted from a unilateral act designating a beneficiary[95]. In English law, the trust is not a contractual arrangement[96] like it is in Colombia. There is a historical distinction, in English law where contracts were created by the Common law Courts and trust was created by Equity[97].

In the English law, a contract can be one way of delivering the benefits of property to another[98], supposing that the trust was a contract between the settlor and the trustee, they would be able to revoke or modify it at any time and the beneficiary would not have enforceable action. But with the trust, after its formation, the settlor has no further interest or action, it is irrevocable and only the beneficiary can enforce it[99].

Some are of the thought that English Trust are contracts; for John H Langbein *'The trust straddles our categories of property and contract, because it embodies a contract about how property is to be deployed. [...] my purpose in emphasizing the contractarian basis of the trust is to account for the trust more accurately'*[100].

In Colombia, the trust is a contract, in which one person in charges another to meet a specific purpose in relation to specific assets, whose ownership will transmit in order to enable him to fulfil the intended purpose, in favour of one or more beneficiaries[101]. In other words, it involves the transfer of ownership to the trustee to establish an autonomous estate[102] which he holds. According to the Colombian

---

[95] MA Carregal, *El fideicomiso: Regulación jurídica y posibilidades prácticas* (Editorial Universidad de Buenos Aires 1982) 34.

[96] Wilson v Lord Bury and Others [1879-80] LR 5 QBD 518 by Brett LJ.

[97] PH Pettit, *Equity and the Law of Trusts*, (11th edn, Oxford University Press 2009) 31.

[98] S Wilson, *Todd & Wilson's textbook on trusts* (10th edn, Oxford University Press 2011) 45.

[99] Ibid., 46.

[100] JH Langbein, 'The Contractarian Basis of the Law of Trusts', [1995-1996] 105 Yale LJ 625.

[101] JA Arrubla Paucar, *Contratos Mercantiles Tomo IV* (Biblioteca Jurídica Diké 2009) 152.

[102] Article 1226 Commercial Code of Colombia 1971.

D. General Differences about the trust

Commercial Code, the commercial trust is a legal transaction whereby one person, called 'settlor' transfers one or more specified goods to a 'trustee', who agrees to manage it to fulfil a specific purpose set by the settlor for his own benefit or to benefit a third party named 'beneficiary'[103]; the same person can be both the settlor and the beneficiary and only credit institutions and trust companies, especially authorised by the Financial Superintendence may have the quality of fiduciary[104].

As we have said, in Colombia it is a plurilateral agreement, because it is formed by three parties and for two of them arise obligations at the moment when the contract is made, for the settlor and the trustee. The beneficiary has expectations and is bound to respect the contract in its entirety[105]. The legal entitlement of the beneficiary does not involve any direct relationship with the assets of the trust[106] and the acceptance of the beneficiary is not required[107].

If in Colombia there is a breach of trust, the trustee will be compelled to respond to ordinary negligence[108]. According to the Commercial Code, he has to diligently perform all acts necessary to achieve the purpose of the trust[109]. This will be further explained with more detail when studying the liability of the trustee.

There are some similarities between the English trust and a contract like the personal obligations between the parties, but there are major distinctions like the ones pointed by Hudson *'First, a trust creates proprietary rights in favour of the beneficiaries and is therefore not restricted to personal claims for compensation. Secondly, the obligations which arise in a contract are created by the common intention of the parties, whereas the trust obligations arise because equity acts on the conscience of the trustee [...]. Thirdly, trusts impose fiduciary obligations in relation to specific property whereas contracts ordinarily do not'*.[110]

---

[103] Ibid.
[104] Ibid.
[105] JA Arrubla Paucar, *Contratos Mercantiles Tomo IV* (Biblioteca Jurídica Diké 2009) 154.
[106] M Lupoi, *Trusts: A Comparative Study* (Cambridge University Press 2001) 321.
[107] Ibid.
[108] Article 1234 Commercial Code of Colombia 1971.
[109] Ibid.
[110] A Hudson, *Equity and trusts*, (6th edn, Routledge-Cavendish 2010) 68.

Applying the theory to *Foskett v McKeown*[111] one of the essential features of trust for not being a contract in the English law, is the possibility in case of breach of trust of recovering the assets or obtaining the compensation for the same value[112]. I belive that this is related with the fact that the majority of the House of the Lords decided that the purchasers had a right on the policy for the amount of the premiums that were paid with the stolen money as they assured that they were able to trace it[113]. According to the Colombian law in the case of sums of money that are delivered to the trustee, from the moment they enter into the agreement, he becomes owner of that money[114], and this is why the purchasers would be entitled to the return of their money with interests, but not to any rights on the policy. A different consequence will occur if the trust property was not money, if it was a specific good in which case the trustee would be compelled to restitute the exact same object if possible. However with the money, according to the provisions of the Colombian Civil Code, the trustee at the end of the trust has the obligation to restitute equal sums to the monies transferred from the settlor to him, although it is presumed that he is allowed to use them as long as he repays them at the end[115].

III. Delegation of Trustee's powers

In Colombian law, one of the fundamental duties of the trustee with the beneficiaries is not to delegate to third parties the trust administration or execution of acts to be directly performed by him[116]. This is because in Colombia, the trust is a contract *intuito personae*, which means that the trustee has been especially chosen by the settlor and is the only one that can perform the administration of the trust directly as these contracts are held in special regard to the person[117]. The Commercial Code, when referring to the duties of the trustee qualifies them as non-

---

[111] Foskett v McKeown [2001] 1 AC 102 (HL).
[112] Ibid.
[113] Ibid.
[114] Article 1226 Commercial Code of Colombia 1971.
[115] Article 2246 Civil Code of Colombia.
[116] JA Arrubla Paucar, *Contratos Mercantiles Tomo IV* (Biblioteca Jurídica Diké 2009) 157.
[117] Ibid.

delegable[118]. Although, the academics have argued that it must be admitted that in certain circumstances, and given certain discretionary acts, the trustee must be understood authorised to delegate[119].

The academics have held that this general rule may not be so absolute in Colombia for the following reasons[120]:

(i) In Colombia, only a legal person may be a trustee and therefore the employees working for said entity can act in accordance with their requests.

(ii) There are certain obligations under the trust that must necessarily be in the hands of third parties such as the appraisal of real estate and legal representation.

(iii) The consultative or advisory committees that are provided in the trust agreements, does not shift the responsibility of the trustee.

Regarding to this, in English law under the old case law, a trustee could not delegate her obligations as a trustee according to the principle *delegates non potest delegare*[121]. Although, currently there are some circumstances in which the trustees can delegate their duties appointing agents, custodians and nominees; these are: (i) when the appointees carry on business in that capacity, or are body corporate controlled by the trustees, (ii) if the delegates are a body corporate recognised under s 9 of the Administration of Justice Act 1985[122]. The Trustee Act 2000, states a provision about the powers of trustees to delegate a person to exercise their delegable functions[123], and brings a list of the functions that cannot be delegated in s 11(2) that are: the functions related to the distribution of the assets of the trust, the power to decide if a payment out of the trust found should be made out of income or capital, the power to appoint a person to be a trustee and any power to delegate responsibilities or functions that he has as a trustee[124].

---

[118] Article 1234 Commercial Code of Colombia 1971. The Colombian Code of Commerce in this provision, introduces a list of the non-delegable duties of the trustee, in addition to those provided in the trust instrument.

[119] JA Arrubla Paucar, *Contratos Mercantiles Tomo IV* (Biblioteca Jurídica Diké 2009) 174.

[120] Ibid.

[121] A Hudson, *Equity and trusts*, (6th edn, Routledge-Cavendish 2010) 320.

[122] Ibid., 438.

[123] S 11 Trustee Act 2000.

[124] S 11(2) Trustee Act 2000.

Both legislations might have similar practical effects in this respect, but the English one is more exact than the Colombian one. It is clear that in the Colombian law, despite the regulation of the Commercial Code, according to which the trustee is precluded downloading full responsibility on a third party in the administration of the trust, it is necessary to recognise that in certain circumstances, like the ones mentioned above, the trustee might be able to delegate. In the English law, these circumstances that allow the trustee to delegate are clearly set in the Trustee Act 2000, I submit that this gives the parties more certainty and legal security than in the Colombian case.

IV. Duty to avoid conflicts of interests and not to earn unauthorised profits

In Colombia, the fundamental duty of the trustee with the beneficiary is the loyalty, if there is a conflict of interest with the trustee, this one shall always act in the interest of the trust[125]. According to this, all profits made by the trustee should be for the trust, and his personal interest must give way to the beneficiaries' interests. There are some activities of the trustees in general, where they have complementary duties, as stated in the Colombia Commercial Code, as to maintain the trust assets separate from their own, the transfer of property to the beneficiary in their time, provide information and accountabilities[126] among others.

In relation to this duty, in English law, the trustee has as well an obligation to avoid conflicts of interest[127] either between two fiduciary duties, or between his personal interests and the interests of the beneficiary[128]. The idea of this disposition is to prevent abuse of the fiduciary position by imposing this duty to the trustee and avoid actual and potential conflicts of interest[129].

In *Chan v Zacharia*, there is a position that states: '*Stated comprehensively in terms of the liability to account, the principle of equity is that a person who is under a fiduciary obligation must account to the person to whom the obligation is owed for any benefit or gain (i) which*

---

[125] Article 1234 n6 Commercial Code of Colombia 1971.
[126] Article 1234 Commercial Code of Colombia 1971.
[127] A Hudson, *Equity and trusts*, (6th edn, Routledge-Cavendish 2010) 321.
[128] Ibid., 334.
[129] Ibid.

has been obtained or received in circumstances where a conflict or significant possibility of conflict existed between his fiduciary duty and his personal interest in the pursuit or possible receipt of such a benefit or gain or (ii) which was obtained or received by use or by reason of his fiduciary position or of opportunity or knowledge resulting from it'[130].

This refers to: (i) 'No conflict rule' prohibits fiduciaries from allowing any conflict between their personal interests and the fiduciary duties, and the (ii) 'No profit rule' prohibits fiduciaries from obtaining any profit from their fiduciary offices[131].

The only way of exonerating the trustee from liability would be demonstrating that it was authorised to act the way she did[132]. There could be a conflict of interest in the event that the trustee makes any unauthorised profits from the trust, defrauding the trust by abstracting profits to themselves[133], and there is another case of self-dealing transactions, where the trustee purports to deal on her own account with the trust property[134], eg buying assets of the trust at an advantageous price.

In *Foskett v McKeown*[135] the trustee breached this obligation of avoiding conflicts of interest when in breach of trust used the money of the purchasers to pay two annual premiums of the insurance policy, this and the fact that as a trustee of two separate funds mixed the funds, affecting two innocent parties the purchasers and the children. Lord Millet held '*In the present case the plaintiffs' be neficial interest plainly bound Mr Murphy, a trustee who wrongfully mixed the trust money with his own and whose every dealing with the money (including the payment of the premiums) was in breach of trust*'[136]. Accordingly, we can say that in Colombian law here we have a clear breach of this duty that is expressly regulated in the Code of Commerce[137]; And in English law this wrongdoing of the trustee will breach the 'no conflict rule'.

In general terms, it is possible to say that both systems agree on this duty for the trustee of avoiding conflicts of interest, which can

---

[130] Chan v Zacharia (1984) 154 CLR 178, 199, Don King Productions Inc v Warren [2000] Ch 291.

[131] A Hudson, *Equity and trusts*, (6th edn, Routledge-Cavendish 2010) 335.

[132] Ibid.

[133] Ibid.

[134] Ibid., 337.

[135] Foskett v McKeown [2001] 1 AC 102 (HL).

[136] Ibid. by Millet LJ.

[137] Article 1233 Commercial Code of Colombia 1971.

be associated in turn with the principle of good faith, except that in this last aspect there are certain discrepancies in both legal systems as further explained.

V. The Principle of Good Faith

We can link the duty of avoiding conflicts of interest with the duty of acting in good faith, as both of them are related. The principle of good faith has a strong regulation in the Colombian law, that includes all the contractual relationships and is binding for the parties even before the agreement is made[138]. However, in English law if parties agree to good faith it will be enforced, but there is no general duty to negotiate in good faith as in Colombian law. According to *Petromec Inc v Petroleo Brasileiro*[139] one of the leading cases in this topic that introduces the reasons not to enforce the good faith in English law, and the reasons are:

> '(1) that the obligation is an agreement to agree and thus too uncertain to enforce, (2) that it is difficult, if not impossible, to say whether, if negotiations are brought to an end, the termination is brought about in good or in bad faith, and (3) that, since it can never be known whether good faith negotiations would have produced an agreement at all or what the terms of any agreement would have been if it would have been reached, it is impossible to assess any loss caused by breach of the obligation'[140]

In the Colombian legal system, there are duties that bind the parties even from the pre-contract stage, that is to say, even before the contract of trust the trustee is compelled to act in good faith following the provision of the Commercial Code referred above. Cooperation and loyalty are parameters to determine when the performance of the parties has been against the principle of good faith. According to the Civil legislation in Colombia, and following a principle of the Roman law, the good faith is presumed[141].

---

[138] Article 863 Commercial Code of Colombia 1971.

[139] Petromec Inc v Petroleo Brasileiro S A Petrobras [2007] EWCA Civ 1371; [2008] CP Rep 16.

[140] Petromec Inc v Petroleo Brasileiro S A Petrobras [2005] EWCA Civ 891 at 116 by Longmore LJ.

[141] Article 769 Colombian Civil Code.

D. General Differences about the trust

This is an important difference between both systems before the creation of the trust, as we know, in the English law the trust is not a contract[142], and even if it was, there is no obligation for the parties to act in good faith in the negotiations[143] as explained above. However, in Colombia there is express regulation in the Commercial Code, according to which the parties have to act in good faith before entering in the agreement, the trustee is required to act in good faith with a special duty of care, not only to the future settlor, but with potential and future beneficiaries of the trust[144].

Things get different after the trust is made, there is an interesting approach of the English law in which the case law mentions the good faith as an obligation for the fiduciary. Lord Millet talks about the loyalty as essence of the fiduciary relationship in *Bristol and West Building Society v Mothew,* where he held that '*A fiduciary must act in good faith; he must not make a profit out of his trust; he must not place himself in a position where his duty and his interest may conflict; he may not act for his own benefit or the benefit of a third person without the informed consent of his principal*'[145]. The principle of good faith is expressly recognised in the case law for the fiduciary, as an obligation to avoid conflicts of interest, and this case has been followed more recently by *Sinclair Investments v Versailles*[146] and other cases that acknowledge the significance of good faith in the trust.

Applying this to *Foskett v McKeown* [147] the trustee breached his duty of good faith according to the English law, when he was acting for his own good without taking in account the interests of the beneficiaries, taking the trust money for his own benefit, or to be more specific for the benefit of the ones who received the life insurance policy after he committed suicide. In Colombia, he clearly breached the good faith and this is inseparable of his liability; according to the law, this will be grounds for removal of the trustee.[148]

---

[142] J Mowbray, L Tucker, N Le Poidevin, E Simpson and J Brightwell, *Lewin on Trusts* (18th edn, Sweet & Maxwell 2011) 1-01.

[143] Petromec Inc v Petroleo Brasileiro SA Petrobras [2007] EWCA Civ 1371; [2008] CP Rep 16.

[144] Article 863 Commercial Code of Colombia 1971.

[145] Bristol and West Building Society v Mothew [1998] Ch 1 by Lord Millet LJ.

[146] Sinclair Investments (UK) Ltd v Versailles Trade Finance Ltd [2011] 3 WLR 1153, Item Software (UK) Ltd v Fassihi [2005] ICR 450.

[147] Foskett v McKeown [2001] 1 AC 102 (HL).

[148] Article 1239 n3 Commercial Code of Colombia 1971.

It is submitted that 'good faith' is not a proper consideration of English fiduciary law, however it is defined[149]. For Rebecca Lee, regardless of this, if the trustee acts in 'good faith' this is not sufficient to exonerate him from the breach of another fiduciary duty, since the fact that the fiduciary has been acting honestly does not necessarily means that is avoiding conflicts of interest[150].

In this respect there is an important difference with the Colombian law. Colombian law requires the trustee to act in good faith in all the stages of the trust, and the principle of good faith covers all sort of liability for acts against the trust property; we could say that it comprises all sort of responsibility for the trustee's acts, and every time the trustee breaches one of his duties, he would be acting against this principle. I argue that the Colombian approach is more protective of the rights of the beneficiaries. This will be explained in more detail below.

VI. The Trustee's liability

In the Colombian legal system, every event of contractual liability is due to the frustration of the result, and there is a tendency to consider this as an obvious truth that admits no discussion[151], to clarify the debate of liability on the contract of trust, there are some parameters identified by the academics.

The trustee when managing the trust, is bound to exercise care and skill that a man of ordinary prudence would use in managing his own assets; the duty of good faith is called to reclaim the trustee, that special diligence which apparently escapes by the immaturity of the Colombian commercial Law, which was referred to a liability by fault[152].

In Colombia there is a triple division of negligence as further explained: (i) Gross negligence: conscious and voluntary disregard, when there was no due care in the work to be executed or in business of third parties which were given[153]. (ii) Ordinary negligence: failure to exercise reasonable care, when there was lack of diligence in the ordi-

---

[149]R Lee 'Rethinking the content of the fiduciary obligation' [2009] Conv 3, 236.
[150]Ibid.
[151]JA Arrubla Paucar, *Contratos Mercantiles Tomo IV* (Biblioteca Jurídica Diké 2009) 167.
[152]Ibid., 169.
[153]Article 63 Civil Code of Colombia.

nary course of business by the person[154]. (iii) Slight negligence: lack of that careful diligence that a wise man used in the management of his important business[155].

This means that in the Colombian trust, the trustee shall be responsible until the ordinary negligence. According to this, he is liable for gross negligence and ordinary negligence, which has been criticised. The academics have argued that this exempts the trustee from slight negligence, when the idea of the trust is to delegate him the management of the assets, seems bizarre that he is not required by law to perform the task with the careful diligence that a wise man used in the management of his important business[156]. They advocate for a trend that should be to move away from the tripartite conception of liability based on the role of the general principle of good faith, which can lead us to reformulate the contractual liability, filling the spaces with a special and professional duty of care which necessarily requires the utmost diligence[157].

In English law, there is a duty for the trustee to exercise reasonable care[158], that would be the legal equivalent for the disposition explained afore in the Colombian system. In *Speight v Gaunt* Lord Blackburn held '*as a general rule a trustee sufficiently discharges his duty if he takes in managing trust affairs all those precautions which an ordinary prudent man of business would take in managing similar affairs of his own*'[159].

Apart from the case law, the duty of care has been object of statutory regulation by the Trustee Act 2000 which in section 1 provides[160]:

> (1) Whenever the duty under this subsection applies to a trustee, he must exercise such care and skill as is reasonable in the circumstances, having regard in particular
>
> (a) to any special knowledge or experience that he has or holds himself out as having, and
>
> (b) if he acts as trustee in the course of a business or profession, to any special knowledge or experience that it is

---

[154] Ibid.
[155] Ibid.
[156] JA Arrubla Paucar, *Contratos Mercantiles Tomo IV* (Biblioteca Jurídica Diké 2009) 169.
[157] Ibid., 170.
[158] Trustee Act 2000.
[159] Speight v Gaunt [1883] 9 AC 1.
[160] S 1(1) Trustee Act 2000.

reasonable to expect of a person acting in the course of that kind of business or profession.

At this point we can see a clear difference in the English and Colombian law on trust. According to the case law, in English law the trustee is responsible for what we would call in Colombia 'slight negligence'[161], the third form of negligence mentioned above, which requires from the trustee utmost diligence and care. In Colombia the trustee is just liable for an ordinary negligence, which is not sufficient. The English approach is better; I submit that it provides a higher degree of legal security in the figure of trust.

In Colombia, the trustee is not liable for any loss suffered by the heritage. That responsibility must necessarily result from a breach of the contract. The Trust, therefore, is not an insurer of goods, and therefore only responds when it has failed to comply with their obligations: if the loss is not due to lack of care and prudence from the trustee or any other breach of its contractual commitments, there is no obligation to indemnify[162]. Although, when celebrating the agreement the parties can pact that the trustee would compensate them for exceptional cases where ordinarily he would not be liable.

In Colombian law, the trustee is liable for breach of the contract of trust, whether intentionally or recklessly he violates any of his obligations, either by action or omission. He is also guilty if the quality of their performance does not reach the minimum level required or if one of his officers or employees causes damage to the trust assets[163].

In the English law, the case law establishes the liability of the trustee. In the old cases like *Learoyd v Whiteley*, Lord Watson held '*Business men of ordinary prudence may, and frequently do, select investments which are more or less of a speculative character; but it is the duty of a trustee to confine himself to the class of investments which are permitted by the trust, and likewise to avoid all investments of that class which are attended with hazard.*'[164], this particular case points out that the trustee not only shall have the standard care of a prudent businessperson, but must also avoid all the investments of hazardous nature.

---

[161] Article 63 Civil Code of Colombia.
[162] JA Arrubla Paucar, *Contratos Mercantiles Tomo IV* (Biblioteca Jurídica Diké 2009) 163.
[163] Ibid.
[164] Learoyd v Whiteley [1887] LR 12 AC 727.

D. General Differences about the trust

This conception has changed and developed in the case law, since nowadays all the investments and business represent a risk. In *Bartlett v Barclays Bank* a distinction was made between the hazard and a prudent degree of risk, Lord Brightman stated: '*The distinction is between a prudent degree of risk on the one hand, and hazard on the other. Nor must the court be astute to fix liability upon a trustee who has committed no more than an error of judgment, from which no business man, however prudent, can expect to be immune*'[165].

It is interesting how English law does not make a distinction between negligence, in which it differs from civil law systems, as explained in the case law, where in *Goodman v. Harvey*, Lord Denman held '*Gross negligence may be evidence of mala fides, but is not the same thing*'.[166] On the other hand, the Colombian Civil Code states that the gross negligence in the civil matters tantamount to intent, which is to infer the positive intention of harm the person or property of another[167].

If we bring *Foskett v McKeown*[168] to explain the liability of the trustee according to the Colombian law, we can say that in the division explained afore, he would be responsible for gross negligence. As it is summarised in chapter A, Murphy breached the trust wrongfully stealing money from the purchasers to pay the last premiums of his last insurance and then committed suicide; the facts demonstrate that his acts were conscious and voluntary which in Colombian law equates to the intent.

In the former case, the problem of the trustee according to the Colombian laws, will be for fraudulent bad management. If the trustee was acting against the terms established in the trust instrument or against the purpose of the trust, he is liable and compromises his own property, with those affected by his illegal actions. In Colombian law he who causes damage is called to compensate, being the basis of that the contractual liability.

Therefore, the purchasers will have the right to claim the money stolen from the trust for concept of damages,[169] and the interests of this money for the concept of lost profits.[170] There is a causal bond

---

[165] Bartlett and Others v Barclays Bank Trust Co Ltd [1980] Ch 515 by Brightman LJ.
[166] Goodman v Harvey and Others [1836] 4 A & E 870, 876 by Lord Denman CJ.
[167] Article 63 Civil Code of Colombia.
[168] Foskett v McKeown [2001] 1 AC 102 (HL).
[169] Article 1613 Civil Code of Colombia.
[170] Ibid.

according to which the illegal action of the trustee caused damage to the purchasers – the beneficiaries –, and he had the intention of using the trust property for his own benefit which was paying the premiums of the life insurance, even when after that he died by his own hand.

VII. The validity of exclusion of liability clauses in English law

Can the contract of trust contain clauses exonerating the trustee of liability? According to the Colombian Civil law, is not possible to condone the future intent, it is not valid[171]. The contractual provision against such a prohibition would face the law and order and would be void for illegality of object. As mentioned above, under the principle of good faith, the trustee is bound to any degree of liability and therefore would be no valid in Colombian law, a clause that seeks to exonerate him from liability[172].

In English law, there is a big difference in this aspect; the trustee has a right to exclude their liability by express provision in the trust instrument[173], which means that the trustee's liability for breach of trust can be limited or completely excluded if there is an express provision for this in the trust instrument[174]. To prevent the trustee from being liable for certain acts or omissions. This is stated in the law as follows:

In the English law, if the trustee has acted according to his duties, would be protected. The leading case in this area is the decision in *Armitage v Nurse*, Lord Millett stated that '*A trustee who is guilty of such conduct either consciously takes a risk that loss will result, or is recklessly indifferent whether it will or not. If the risk eventuates he is personally liable. But if he consciously takes the risk in good faith and with the best intentions, honestly believing that the risk is one which ought to be taken in the interests of the beneficiaries, there is no reason why he should not be protected by an exemption clause which excludes liability for wilful default*'[175].

---

[171] Article 1522 Civil Code of Colombia.

[172] JA Arrubla Paucar, *Contratos Mercantiles Tomo IV* (Biblioteca Jurídica Diké 2009) 176.

[173] A Hudson, *Equity and trusts*, (6th edn, Routledge-Cavendish 2010) 371.

[174] Ibid.

[175] Armitage v Nurse and Others [1998] Ch 241 by Lord Millett LJ.

This case, excludes the trustee's personal liability for all causes and breaches of trust except for fraud. This differs from the Colombian legislation where as mentioned above, it is not possible to validly introduce one of these clauses in the contract of trust, limiting or excluding the liability of the trustee, a clause to exempt trustees from liability would be void and null. *Armitage v Nurse*, held that a clause would be valid excluding the trustee's personal liability in all situations including loss caused by the trustee's own gross negligence[176].

In relation to this, when there is a loss in Colombian law, it does not affect the estate of the trustee, because this is an independent estate, and the trustee has to assume the loss with the trust, unless he acted in a negligent way, unlike in English law, in Colombia, the trustee does not have the possibility of validly include exclusion of liability clauses in the contract of trust. This is introduced in the Commercial Code of Colombia according to which for all legal purposes, the trust assets should be separated from the rest of the assets of the trustee and to those belonging to other fiduciary business and will form an autonomous estate created for the purposes referred to in the contract of trust[177].

The trustee has the duty of transferring the of goods of the contract of trust to its termination, as the Colombia Supreme Court has held[178] in this case one must distinguish between the transfer of sums of money and the transfer of certain bodies. In the case where sums of money were delivered by the settlor to the trustee, the trustee is the owner, not only under the provisions of section 1226 of the Commercial Code but also under the principles governing gender obligations[179] arising from contracts of deposit and mandate. According to this, the trustee owes the money but has the duty of returning the same amount to the beneficiary at the termination of the contract. In the case of the loss of a true body that had been transferred by the settlor to the trustee, the loss is to be assumed by the trustee, but it only affects the autonomous heritage, unless the trustee has not taken the care required by law, does not have to put his general estate, to account for the loss[180].

---

[176] A Hudson, *Equity and trusts*, (6th edn, Routledge-Cavendish 2010) 372.
[177] Article 1233 Commercial Code of Colombia 1971.
[178] Judgment of the Supreme Court of Colombia, 9th August 1995 by JT Jaramillo.
[179] Article 2246 Civil Code of Colombia.
[180] Judgment of the Supreme Court of Colombia, 9th August 1995 by JT Jaramillo.

The Colombian approach offers a better protection to the beneficiaries, however, in English law The Law Commission has expressed concern about this issue. In the Law Commission Report 'Trustee Exception Clauses' of 2006, it was held that the possibility of having exclusion of liability clauses in English law is not giving adequate protection to the beneficiaries. The Commission argued: *'we remain of the view that the current law governing trustee exemption clauses is capable of causing unfairness and should be addressed'*[181]. Their particular concerned is when this clauses are included and the settlor does not fully understand their meaning and effect, jeopardising the reliance on the terms of the trust.

VIII. Remuneration for the performance of the trustee

According to the Colombian Code of Commerce, the trustee shall ensure maximum performance of the property subject to the trust business, for which any disposition is always onerous and for profit, unless contrary determination of the contract[182].

The obligation of loyalty in English trust, is distinguishing the character of fiduciary relationships, it determines whether equity recognises a relationship as fiduciary[183]. For the trustee is ensuring that they are not motivated by anything but the interests of the beneficiary, and the trustee is not entitled to make any profit or benefit from the fiduciary position[184].

In *Bray v Ford*, Lord Herschell stated: *'It is an inflexible rule of a Court of Equity that a person in a fiduciary position, such as the respondent's is not, unless otherwise expressly provided, entitled to make a profit; he is not allowed to put himself in a position where his interest and duty conflict. It does not appear to me that this rule is, as has been said, founded upon principles of morality'*[185].

The existence of this principle, leads to the thinking that in English law trustees are not allowed or entitled to charge remuneration

---

[181]Trustee Exception Clauses 2006. The Law Commission (LAW COM No 301).
[182]Article 1234 n6 Commercial Code of Colombia 1971.
[183]S Wilson, *Todd & Wilson's textbook on trusts* (10th edn, Oxford University Press 2011) 340.
[184]Ibid., 341.
[185]George Bray v John Rawlinson Ford [1896] A C 44, by Lord Herschell LJ.

D. General Differences about the trust

for their performance[186]. If we follow that interpretation the English system would differ from the Colombian law, where the trust is an onerous contract and the payment of the fees is set by the Financial Superintendence[187]. In English law there is a statutory provision contained in the Trustee Act 2000 according to which the trustee is entitled to payment if *'(a) there is a provision in the trust instrument entitling him to receive payment out of trust funds in respect of services provided by him to or on behalf of the trust, and (b) the trustee is a trust corporation or is acting in a professional capacity'*[188].

At this point there is a difference in both legal systems, the fees object of payment for the trustees in the Colombian legislation are established by the Financial Superintendence[189], which is an Organ through which the President of Colombia exercise 'inspection, monitoring and control over the persons involved in financial activities, securities, insurance, and any other related to the management, use or investment of resources collected from the public'[190].

In this regard, we have that in Colombia, the economic function that meets the trust is to give confidence to the parties to conduct their legal business. It is the presence of the trustee, as a specialised entity monitored by state authorities in charge of observing the financial activity, which gives comfort to the parties to the business that they tend.

Although, at the same time, the remuneration of the trustee must be a specific space for the exercise of the autonomy of the will, where the parties must freely agree what the compensation of the trustee should be. It seems to be very inconvenient to leave this sort of authority to the Financial Superintendence. In terms of obligations and contracts it is important to have stable legislation to create a trusting environment for international and Colombian entrepreneurs to conduct their operations. There is no sense in letting the Financial Superintendence an assignment of this nature.

---

[186] S Wilson, *Todd & Wilson's textbook on trusts* (10th edn, Oxford University Press 2011) 342.

[187] JA Arrubla Paucar, *Contratos Mercantiles Tomo IV* (Biblioteca Jurídica Diké 2009) 155.

[188] S 28 Trustee Act 2000.

[189] Article 1237 Commercial Code of Colombia 1971.

[190] Financial Superintendence of Colombia, www.superfinanciera.gov.co accessed 8th August 2012.

In Colombia, the trustee is entitled to remuneration for his performance by whoever requests him. The original text of the Colombian Code of Commerce included a fee regime for the trust to be set up by the Financial Superintendence. This has been a polemic subject in the doctrine that considers that there is nothing more absurd than introducing a straitjacket to an activity such as ductile as the commercial trust and the parties must freely agree what should be the compensation of the trustee[191]. Fortunately, this power of the body of control – The Superintendence – has been handled with care and in the practice has allowed the parties to manage their own rates[192].

IX. Duty of the trustee with the trust property

According to the Colombian law, in the contract of trust, the results of the management carried out by the trustee, are not for its profit but for other parties of the contract[193]. The Financial Superintendence held that, given that the duties of the trustee are of medium and not of result, trust companies shall express it visible in the agreements they make for the purpose, moreover, they shall not guarantee a performance for the money received[194].

In the English law, the trustee has a duty of safeguarding the trust property, and preventing any harm to any property that they hold on trust[195]. One of the duties of the trustee is to not simply watch over the property and preserve it from decay but to safeguard the trust property and maintain its utility so it is fit for the purpose[196].

While in the English law the trustee has to think in which way would invest the trust money should be invested, when the Colombian law makes the distinction between obligations of medium and result, what it means is that the trustees should put all their diligence and care in the smooth running of the administration of the trust, but they are not bound to concrete results. This way, if the obligation of the

---

[191] JA Arrubla Paucar, *Contratos Mercantiles Tomo IV* (Biblioteca Jurídica Diké 2009) 155.
[192] Ibid., 222
[193] Ibid., 229.
[194] Resolution 3914 of 1986 Banking Superintendence of Colombia.
[195] A Hudson, *Equity and trusts*, (6th edn, Routledge-Cavendish 2010) 324.
[196] Ibid., 324.

trustee is e.g. to acquire shares in a company and it then suffers losses that reduce the value of the shares, then, these losses are bear by the trustee only as long as a showing of negligence on his part, as regulated in the Colombian legislation[197].

In English law, the trustees have some powers for the administration of the property, but they are not unlimited. They are compelled to manage the trust property in the interests of the beneficiaries. The trustee's authority is ordinarily limited to the doing of acts required or authorised by the general law, as extended by statute, or by the trust instrument[198], and if there is a breach of trust, the trustee is liable as stated in case law *'If specific restitution of the trust property is not possible, then the liability of the trustee is to pay sufficient compensation to the trust estate to put it back to what it would have been had the breach not been committed'*[199].

In Colombia, when administrating the trust property, the trustee has a special duty of disclosure to third parties about the reality of the trust and the capacity in which he operates. The reasons for this is that it is their duty to keep the trust property separate from his property and other businesses that belong to other fiduciaries, here the trust assets are not part of the general guarantee of its creditors and the trust property is only responsible for the obligations contracted in the fulfilment of the purpose of the trust[200].

Bringing this theory to *Foskett v McKeown*,[201] it is clear that in neither of the systems object of comparison in this study, – regardless of the freedom for the administration that the trustee could have –, he will never be allowed to use the trust property for his own expenses and benefit, especially under the circumstances given in this case where the trustee stole the money fraudulently for the payment of the premiums on policy of his life insurance.

In English law this act constitutes breach of trust and in Colombian law breach of contract. This case is a clear example related to

---

[197] Article 2144 Civil Code of Colombia and Article 1243 Commercial Code of Colombia 1971.

[198] J Mowbray, L Tucker, N Le Poidevin, E Simpson and J Brightwell, *Lewin on Trusts* (18th edn, Sweet & Maxwell 2011) 36-01.

[199] Target Holdings Ltd v Redferns [1996] AC 421 at 434 by Lord Browne-Wilkinson LJ, following Nocton v Lord Ashburton [1914] AC 932.

[200] JA Arrubla Paucar, *Contratos Mercantiles Tomo IV* (Biblioteca Jurídica Diké 2009).

[201] Foskett v McKeown [2001] 1 AC 102 (HL).

the duties of the trustee with the trust property. As mentioned afore in this section, in English law the powers of the trustee on the trust property are limited to be on the interest of the beneficiaries, likewise in Colombia. We can say that both laws agree on this principle that was violated by the trustee, although in practice the case would be decided differently.

E. Comparisons

I have compared the English and Colombian trust in nine different elements, with a particular focus on breach of trust. As a general conclusion for this study, I argue that both systems protect the beneficiaries albeit in a different way, nevertheless, in the case of breach of trust, the equitable proprietary rights of the beneficiaries in the English law[202] product of the simultaneous existence in Equity[203]; provide them with a special protection and mechanisms to prevent the trustee from abusing his position, eg the method of tracing.[204] On the other hand, in Colombia, the different interpretations of the fiduciary figure from its regulation in the Commercial Code have lead to uncertainty.

---

[202] R Pierce, J Stevens and W Barr, *The law of trusts and equitable obligations* (Oxford University Press 2010) 53.

[203] A Hudson, *Equity and trusts*, (6th edn, Routledge-Cavendish 2010) 42.

[204] R Pierce, J Stevens and W Barr, *The law of trusts and equitable obligations* (Oxford University Press 2010) 10.

F. Conclusions

After observing the different aspects of the trust in a comparative law, its economic role, its dynamics in the business world and have penetrated the legal analysis, we could draw the following conclusions and recommendations as a summary of this study.

The trust is claimed to be the most important contribution that English law has made to the world of jurisprudence[205]. The importance of studying the English trust in Civil Law countries, is clearly evidenced in the Hague Convention 1985 where the primary purpose of the Convention belong to the dynamics of common law jurisdictions. The Italian academic Maurizio Lupoi, mentioned that the trust had already been recognized in Civil Law jurisdictions by the jurisprudence without a problem[206].

Nevertheless, it is important to bear in mind that there are some particularities of the Civil Law systems – like the Colombian one – which are different from those set for the English trust model. One of them is the existence of a double jurisdiction and the possibility of having two proprietors of the same thing, one in law and one in equity[207]. It is hard to comprehend in the Civil Law, how does the ownership become separated in the English law; where the legal title passes from the settlor to the trustee, being this the only type of title to property before the creation of the trust and the equitable title just appears after this creation for the beneficiary[208]. This is the main

---

[205] M Dixon and G Griffiths (eds), *Contemporary perspectives on property, equity, and trusts law* (Oxford University Press 2007) 143.

[206] M Lupoi, *Introduzione al TRUSTS: Diritto Inglese, Convenzione dell'Aja, Diritto Italiano* (Giuffre Editore 1994) 125.

[207] JA Arrubla Paucar, *Contratos Mercantiles Tomo IV* (Biblioteca Jurídica Diké 2009) 141.

[208] S Wilson, *Todd & Wilson's textbook on trusts* (10th edn, Oxford University Press 2011) 5.

reason why it is not possible to fully identify the fiduciary figures in both systems and legislations.

Another particularity where the English system differs with the Civil Law systems, as mentioned previously, is the fact that the source of trust in the Colombian law is a contract, also the formalities that are required depending of the nature of the trust property; in the case of Colombia in some cases registered public deed[209]. As long as the current regulation on the trust in the Colombian Code of Commerce, the contractual instrument which we have been discussing, instead of fulfilling its basic function of trust lead to certain activities of entrepreneurs, is sinking in a number of uncertainties and risks that discourage the practice.

It is also a relevant characteristic of the Colombian law, the fact that when the trust have a financial nature, the trustee must be either a Bank or a finance company[210] that are monitored by state authorities with the aim of observing the financial activity[211]. These differences, not only legal and substantial, but cultural and attached to the collective idiosyncrasies, determine that we shall look for the nature of the fiduciary business in sources that nourish the Colombian legal system, its customs and the activities of its society, rather than attempt a transplant that probably will not succeed.

For that reason, the doctrine – when referring to adopting the trust in civil law countries – has said that we should receive the trust, but not exactly as it is in English law, we must receive it sticking to our legal traditions, our way of trade, and our way to act in business life, since what does not respond to the customs, is a dead letter[212]. This is what we mentioned before about the issues of transplanting law, it is taking something unfamiliar and trying to domesticate it; in this process of adapting the foreign institution to the legal traditions of the country, the work of scholars and academics plays a major role, their previous analysis of what is to be adopted, helps to introduce and acclimate the external law and facilitates the understanding of it by recipients.

---

[209] Article 1228 Commercial Code of Colombia 1971.

[210] M Lupoi, *Trusts: A Comparative Study* (Cambridge University Press 2001) 320.

[211] Financial Superintendence of Colombia, www.superfinanciera.gov.co accessed 13th August 2012.

[212] MA Carregal, *El fideicomiso: Regulación jurídica y posibilidades prácticas* (Editorial Universidad de Buenos Aires 1982) 34.

We must recognise that humanity has become increasingly towards the unification of negotiable instruments. The globalisation of the economy and the integration of countries into blocks or regions have also made essential the unification of the contractual instruments that support the business of trade. In the future, the approach between two institutions that come from different legal systems has to be bigger, even nowadays, precisely because commercial law has to take off its limits and constantly keep searching for an approach in the legislation of different countries.

G. Reference List

I. Table of Cases

1. English Cases

Armitage v Nurse and Others [1998] Ch 241

Bartlett and Others v Barclays Bank Trust Co Ltd [1980] Ch 515

Bristol and West Building Society v Mothew [1998] Ch 1

Chan v Zacharia (1984) 154 CLR 178

Don King Productions Inc v Warren [2000] Ch 291

Foskett v McKeown [2001] 1 AC 102 (HL)

George Bray v John Rawlinson Ford [1896] AC 44

Goodman v Harvey and Others [1836] 4 A & E 870

Item Software (UK) Ltd v Fassihi [2005] ICR 450

Learoyd v Elizabeth Whiteley [1887] LR 12 AC 727

Lord Dudley and Ward v The Lady Dowager Dudley [1705] Prec Ch 241

Nocton v Lord Ashburton [1914] AC 932

Petromec Inc v Petroleo Brasileiro S A Petrobras [2007] EWCA Civ 1371; [2008] CP Rep 16

Sinclair Investments (UK) Ltd v Versailles Trade Finance Ltd [2011] 3 WLR 1153

Speight v Gaunt [1883] 9 AC 1

Target Holdings Ltd v Redferns [1996] AC 421

Westdeutsche Landesbank Girozentrale v Islington BC [1996] AC 669

Wilson v Lord Bury and Others [1879-80] LR 5 QBD 518

2. Colombian

Judgment of the Supreme Court of Colombia, 9th August 1995, *per* JT Jaramillo.

Judgement of the Supreme Court of Colombia, 15th July 2008, referencia: C-1100131030061998-00579-01.

II. Text Books

de Arespacochaga J, *El trust, la fiducia y figuras afines* (Marcial Pons Ediciones Jurídicas y Sociales S.A Madrid 2000)

Arrubla Paucar JA, *Contratos Mercantiles Tomo VI* (Biblioteca Jurídica Diké 2009)

Dixon M and Griffiths G (eds), *Contemporary perspectives on property, equity, and trusts law* (Oxford University Press 2007)

Carregal MA, *El fideicomiso: Regulación jurídica y posibilidades prácticas* (Editorial Universidad de Buenos Aires 1982)

Elliot C and Quinn F, *English legal system*, (11th edn, Pearsons 2010)

Ellis J, 'General principles and comparative law' [2011] EJIL 22(4), 949

Goode RM and McKendrick E (eds), *Commercial law* (4th edn, Penguin 2010)

Gravells NP, *Land law: text and materials* (Sweet & Maxwell 2010)

Gray KJ and Gray SF, *Elements of land law* (Oxford University Press 2009)

Hudson A, *Equity and trusts* (6th edn, Routledge-Cavendish 2010)

Jordano Barea JB, *El Negocio Fiduciario* (JM Bosch Editor Barcelona 1959)

Langbein JH, 'The Contractarian Basis of the Law of Trusts' [1995-1996] 105 Yale LJ 625

Lee R, 'Rethinking the content of the fiduciary obligation' [2009] Conv 3, 236

Lepaulle P, *Tratado Teórico y Práctico de los Trust* (Editorial Porrúa S.A 1975)

Lupoi M, *Introduzione al TRUSTS: Diritto Inglese, Convenzione dell'Aju, Diritto Italiano* [1994] (Giuffre Editore)

Lupoi M, *Trusts: A Comparative Study* (Cambridge University Press 2001)

Moffat G, *Trusts law: text and materials* (Cambridge University Press 2009)

Mowbray J, Tucker L, Le Poidevin N, Simpson E and Brightwell J, *Lewin on Trusts* (18th edn, Sweet & Maxwell 2011)

Pettit PH, *Equity and the Law of Trusts*, (11th edn, Oxford University Press 2009)

Pierce R, Stevens J and Barr W, *The law of trusts and equitable obligations* (Oxford University Press 2010)

Ramirez A and Otero H 'An Introduction to Colombian Governmental Institutions and Primary Legal Sources' [2011] Globalex (New York University School of Law)

Sherman C, 'The Romanization of English Law' [1913-1914] 23 Yale LJ 318

Wilson S, *Todd & Wilson's textbook on trusts* (10th edn, Oxford University Press 2011)

III. Colombian Legislation

1887 Civil Code of Colombia (*Código Civil Colombiano*)

1971 Commercial Code of Colombia (*Código de Comercio Colombiano*)

Resolution 3914 of 1986 Banking Superintendence of Colombia

IV. English Statutes

1536 The Statute of Uses (27 Hen 8 c 10)

2000 Trustee Act

2006 Trustee Exception Clauses. The Law Commission (LAW COM No 301).

V. Websites

Financial Superintendence of Colombia,
   www.superfinanciera.gov.co